EXPLORING CAREERS IN
TV AND FILM

Producing in TV and Film

Cavendish
Square

New York

Published in 2019 by Cavendish Square Publishing, LLC
243 5th Avenue, Suite 136, New York, NY 10016

Library of Congress Cataloging-in-Publication Data
Names: Boehme, Gerry.
Title: Producing in TV and film / Gerry Boehme.
Description: New York : Cavendish Square, 2019. | Series: Exploring careers in TV and film |
Includes glossary and index.
Identifiers: ISBN 9781502641403 (pbk.) | ISBN 9781502641410 (library bound) |
SBN 9781502641427 (ebook)
Subjects: LCSH: Motion pictures--Production and direction--Juvenile literature. |
Television programs--Production and direction--Juvenile literature.
Classification: LCC PN1994.5 B64 2019 | DDC 791.43023--dc23

Editorial Director: David McNamara
Editor: Kristen Susienka
Copy Editor: Rebecca Rohan
Associate Art Director: Alan Sliwinski
Designer: Christina Shults
Production Coordinator: Karol Szymczuk
Photo Research: J8 Media

Printed in the United States of America

CONTENTS

Major film productions can involve many people, locations, and types of equipment. This crew is filming in Vancouver, Canada.

CHAPTER ONE

Head of the Team

You settle into your seat, popcorn and soft drink close at hand. The previews and commercials have finished, and the theater lights dim. A message appears on the giant screen, telling you it's time to put on your 3D glasses. The blockbuster movie you've waited for is about to start, and you'll soon know whether it's worth the price of your ticket.

Just before you turn off your phone, a friend texts you with a link to a video that someone just posted on YouTube. It runs less than one minute and isn't very polished, but you think it's hilarious. After forwarding the link to other friends, you put your phone in your pocket and sit back to enjoy the movie.

The Producer

A major Hollywood movie and a short YouTube video may not seem to have much in common, but they're actually more alike than you might think. Sure, the movie may have cost millions of dollars, involved hundreds of people, and taken more than a year to make, while the short video may have been filmed and posted by a teenager for free in just a few seconds.

However, both projects started with a person who had an idea. Then, she or he built a plan to bring their idea to life and show it to an audience.

For big, complicated projects like movies or television shows, the person who takes the concept and builds the plan to take it to the screen is called a producer. The larger the project, the more skills a producer needs to have in order to bring the idea to life.

While no high-school student is likely to produce a major movie or television show, it's easier than ever to start working toward that goal. Digital technology and the internet make it possible for beginners to produce their own videos while gaining the experience they'll need to create even better projects down the road.

Key Player

Many movies and TV shows begin with fancy graphics that swirl into focus with names like Buena Vista, Universal, and Lionsgate, major film or TV studios that supported what you are about to see. Sometimes the names of star performers appear, telling you who will play the major roles in the story. The last title usually identifies the director, the person who charted the movie's creative path. Some directors are as famous as their star actors.

You may not have noticed at the time, but you may have also seen the producer's name up there in the credits. While the director may have been responsible for everything that you see on screen, the producer plays an equally important role in making sure the movie gets shown.

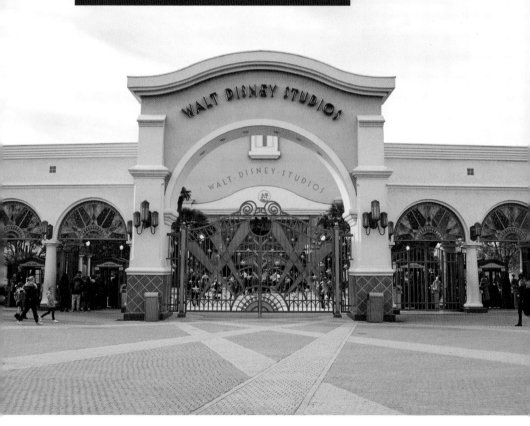

Big Hollywood production companies, like Walt Disney Studios, spend millions of dollars to bring movie blockbusters to the screen.

While a producer's name may not be as familiar, movies and television shows would never get made if not for their hard work and impressive combination of skills. The producer is the jack-of-all-trades who guides a movie or television show from start to finish, from developing the idea and handling the finances to hiring the director and making sure the movie is completed, distributed, and shown.

The Head Coach

John Russo has done it all in the entertainment business. He has written, directed, and/or produced many low-budget, moneymaking feature films, including working with famous director George Romero on the cult horror classic *Night of the Living Dead* in 1968. He has also produced television commercials, educational films, and documentaries, and has published several novels.

Russo admits that it's not easy to explain a producer's role, especially to those outside the industry:

> *There are many types of producer,*
> *with varying degrees of involvement*
> *in the various stages of motion picture*
> *production, which accounts for the*
> *confusion in lay people's minds as to*
> *what, precisely, a producer is supposed*
> *to do. Some producers do little more than*
> *provide the money to make the movie.*
> *Other producers are prime movers during*
> *every phase of a movie from start to finish.*

Tim Fanguy managed video production for the National Basketball Association (NBA) New Orleans Pelicans and for a TV station before building his own video production business. When asked to explain what a producer does, Fanguy said, "The best way to describe the job [is] to use a football reference. The producer is like the head coach and the director is like the quarterback. The producer comes up with the game plan, calls the plays, and the director executes the plan."

Producer Michael Sugar accepted the 2016 Academy Award for Best Picture for the movie *Spotlight*.

A Beginning

Whether it's that movie you paid to see or the YouTube video your friend sent you, no project can begin without a story. Producers find inspiration in many ways. Sometimes they think of an idea themselves, their imagination sparked by a sudden thought, a book, a conversation with a friend, or something they see in a news report. In other cases, a friend or colleague might approach the producer with their own thoughts for a project, perhaps even providing a finished script.

Once the producer decides to start a project, the first step is always to make sure he or she has the legal right to tell the story. If he or she didn't develop the idea, the producer will have his or her lawyers sign a contract with the person who owns it. For example, if the producer wants to use a script or a book that already exists, the producer will take out an option, or a legal contract, that gives him or her the exclusive right for a certain period of time to produce a film or television show based on that work.

Next Steps

If there's no script yet, the producer will hire someone to write it. After that, the producer needs to do the math and figure out how much the project will cost, then go out to find investors willing to pledge enough money to pay all the bills until production is finished and the movie is released. When the necessary funding is secured, it's time to choose the director who will handle all the creative aspects of the project.

A Partnership

Working together, the producer and director build out their dream team of creative and technical professionals. The director then handles the day-to-day moviemaking, while the producer labors in the background, keeping a close eye on the project and making sure it runs smoothly. Even at this early stage, the producer will also start working to set up distribution for the completed film.

If everything goes according to plan and the film is successful, most if not all of the credit will be claimed by the director, actors, writer, composer, and everyone else associated with the creative aspect of the movie. If, on the other hand, the movie bombs—no one sees it or it doesn't make money—the film will be considered a failure, and the producer will suffer most if not all of the blame.

Many Skills

Given all the tasks and that kind of pressure, it's easy to understand why it takes a certain type of person, and a unique set of abilities, to become a producer.

Most people have strengths and weaknesses, and most eventually find jobs that take advantage of their strongest talents. People good at math may choose to enter finance or accounting; those with a knack for language and telling stories might become reporters or novelists. Others may use their cheerful personalities to pursue careers in sales or public relations.

Producers, on the other hand, need to have many strengths and be good at many jobs in order to be successful. Producers don't have to be able to write, direct, edit, or act, but they must be able to help screenwriters, directors, editors, and actors do their best work. They have to understand budgets and numbers, attract investors, and make sure that money is spent wisely and efficiently.

Perhaps most importantly, producers need strong people skills. They have to command the respect of everyone they work with to keep the entire group coordinated and on track, all while managing any conflicts that arise and providing a safe and secure environment. Producers also usually serve as the public face of the project and the main point of contact for everyone outside the production team, including local authorities and the community where shooting takes place.

Like that football coach, producers have to enjoy managing teams, doing many different jobs, and working with all kinds of people, rather than concentrating on just one area.

Starting Early

It's never too soon for students to start thinking about whether a producer's life is right for them. High-school and college programs provide many opportunities to get involved in video production at an early stage, and the digital video capabilities of smartphones and inexpensive cameras make it easier than ever for students to experiment and learn by producing their own projects.

Thinking back to his student experiences, Tim Fanguy remembers:

> The best piece of advice I got was when I was in high school and considering a career in TV. A mentor simply stated, "Be a sponge." What that means is learn everything you can about the business regardless if you want to be on-camera talent, a producer, director [or a] camera operator. You never know what the future holds, and it's best to be well rounded in case your intended career path doesn't work out.

What Fanguy learned about other roles helped shape his career. "When I first started in the business," he continues, "I thought I wanted to be on-air talent, but [I] still learned all of the behind the scenes positions, and quickly realized that being behind the scenes was much more natural and more exciting and fun for me. If I wasn't a sponge early on, who knows where I would be right now."

Start With Questions

Famous producer, director, and writer John Landis began his career in the mailroom of a major studio, 20th Century Fox. After that, he worked as a production assistant, actor, extra, and stuntman before successfully producing, directing, and writing his own projects. Landis gained international fame with movies like *Animal House*, *The Blues Brothers*, and *Trading Places*, and by producing the groundbreaking music video of Michael Jackson's song "Thriller." Landis has also produced and directed television programs and has made commercials for companies like Coca-Cola, Pepsi, Kellogg's, and Disney.

During an interview at the New York Film Institute, Landis was asked for his advice on how to start out as a film producer. Landis responded with a simple answer: "It depends on what you want to do. Why do you really want to do it?"

Before any student begins a video project, he or she should ask themselves why they want to work on it and what their goals are. Do you want to show it to just a few people or many? Are you looking for credit or applause? Do you want to make money, or are you doing it just for fun?

Then, take an honest look at your skills and abilities. What are you good at? What do you like to

This group of film students from Loyola Marymount University School of Film and Television readies a set for filming.

do, and what would you rather have someone else do? Where might you need assistance? Can someone help?

Also, make sure you have the time for the project. Schoolwork, after-school activities and jobs, family obligations, time with friends—there are only so many hours in the day, and everyone also needs time to sleep too!

Great Satisfaction

While it can be difficult, some people think that producers have the best job in film and television. David Mamet, a prize-winning producer, playwright, screenwriter, and director, describes movie workers as:

> *the hardest working and most spirited people it has ever been my pleasure to work with. The spirit on a set is: "Do it right, do it now, help the other guy, enjoy yourself." I love the life on the set ... a bunch of folks get together ... work hard, play hard, sleep a little, and take a lot of pride in seeing the thing through.*

The producer gets to build that group of people and coach the project through from start to finish.

Producers manage all the different areas in film and television projects, including live performers, equipment, sets, and props.

CHAPTER TWO

Working Together

Kevin Feige and Amy Pascal produced the 2017 box office smash *Spider-Man: Homecoming.* When the movie premiered, critic Glenn Kelly, writing on film review site www.rogerebert.com, called it a "comprehensively crowd-pleasing success." Film review website Rotten Tomatoes said that 92 percent of critics gave it a positive review, and 88 percent of its members rated the movie at least 3.5 stars out of four. The film turned out to be one of the biggest box-office successes that summer, making more than $333 million in the United States and nearly $880 million worldwide.

Many Contributors

As the movie ended and music played over the closing credits, most people collected their things, rose from their seats, and headed to the exits. A smaller number may have stayed until the very end, waiting to see if the film included an after-credits scene (also called a tag, stinger, or credit cookie), a short clip that appears after the credits.

While they were waiting, those stragglers may have noticed a series of more than 2,200 names and titles scrolling past, all of them listing members of the extensive and multitalented team that helped bring *Spider-Man: Homecoming* to the screen.

Group Coordinators

As the movie's producers, Feige and Pascal handled all the various phases of film production (see chapter 3), from developing the initial concept, approving the script, and budget preparation to shooting, postproduction, and release. They acted as administrators, communicators, and guides, helping literally thousands of people reach a final goal: completing the film as the director envisioned.

Like other producers, neither Feige nor Pascal acted, directed, or edited. They did have to possess other qualities, however, including understanding the requirements of each role and managing the process to get the best performances from everyone involved.

Blending Talents

Legendary producer Richard Zanuck spent more than fifty years in Hollywood making great movies of all kinds, ranging from *The Sound of Music* to *Cocoon* to *Jaws* to *Planet of the Apes.* Zanuck once said that "the producer is like the conductor in an orchestra. Maybe he can't play every instrument, but he knows what every instrument should sound like."

Kathleen Kennedy is one of the most successful and respected producers and executives in the film industry today. She currently serves as president of Disney's Lucasfilm, and produced *Star Wars: The Force Awakens*, *Rogue One*, and *Star Wars: The Last Jedi*.

Speaking about her role, Kennedy said:

> *The producer in effect has to work as a translator. You form a very tight relationship with the director and writer, from the beginning, and then you are constantly communicating to the various people that begin to come into the process, as you are trying to manage to hold on to a vision that needs to be communicated over a long period of time. You could be working on something for three, four, or five years. Maintaining that vision and point of view is really difficult. Communication skills are key.*

Different Responsibilities

No two producers operate the same way, and individual producers often change their roles based on the requirements of the project they are involved with at that time. Some producers work for themselves and move from project to project. Others are employed by film companies or television stations or networks. Many are paid a fee negotiated with the studio beforehand, or the two sides agree to compensation based on a portion of the film's profits.

Producers may not be as well known or claim as much credit as more visible roles like directors or

WORKING FOR CHANGE

Producers know that teams benefit when they include people with diverse backgrounds and abilities. Unfortunately, many industries, including Hollywood, still fail the diversity test when it comes to recognizing the talents of certain groups, especially women and people of color.

Producer, director, and screenwriter Jeffrey Jacob (J.J.) Abrams wants to change that. Abrams has rolled up almost too many film successes to count, including *Star Wars: The Force Awakens* and *Star Wars: The Last Jedi*. He has also created and executive-produced various television series and cofounded a production company, Bad Robot.

In March 2016, Abrams announced a major initiative to increase diversity in Hollywood and the film industry. Earlier that year, the "#OscarsSoWhite" controversy exploded after people of color were noticeably left off Academy Award ballots despite the great success of many films featuring diverse casts.

Abrams says the #OscarsSoWhite controversy served as his "wake-up call." He decided to partner with leading talent company Creative Artists Agency (CAA), as well as Hollywood studios Warner Bros. and Paramount, to make sure that women and minorities received consideration for writing, directing, and acting jobs at Bad Robot that better reflected their representation in the US population. "We're working to find a rich pool of representative [high-level] talent and give them the opportunity they deserve and we can all benefit from," Abrams

Filmmaker J.J. Abrams is working hard to help improve diversity in the movie business.

told the *Hollywood Reporter*. "It's good for audiences and it's good for the bottom line."

Policies similar to Bad Robot's are now being adopted all over Hollywood.

actors, but without a producer, a movie would never even get off the ground, much less be completed. Some projects are so large or complex that several people receive "producer" recognition. In fact, big movies and television series often credit many different people with a wide variety of production titles.

In addition to Kevin Feige and Amy Pascal, *Spider-Man: Homecoming*'s official listings credit ten other people with some level of "producer" title, including seven executive producers and three coproducers. The film's closing credits list even more producers, including associate producers, assistant producers, and line producers.

Not That Simple

Why are there so many titles, and what makes them different? In simple terms, a producer starts, coordinates, supervises, and controls everything about the film or television project, including the creative approach, hiring the staff, arranging funding, watching the spending, and arranging distribution. In many cases, the producer also develops the idea or script, sometimes working with a writer, and he or she secures the legal right to start the project. Producers usually hire the director and, just as important, the producer develops and oversees the budget.

The producer then coordinates the postproduction work, which includes everything from editing and music to promoting the project to the public. That often includes encouraging the film's stars to talk up the movie on television shows and other public appearances. Sometimes two or more people work as coproducers, reporting to the producer and helping with casting, financing, or postproduction.

Many Levels

In the movie business, an executive producer title often identifies the person who helps raise money for the film but has little to do with the production itself. Executive producers may already be well known in the industry, and some can attract investors just by using their name. Sometimes a co–executive producer title is granted to high-level studio heads or distributors who hold a limited financial stake in the project.

An associate producer performs one or more jobs that a producer assigns. A segment producer produces one or more individual pieces of a project that will include other segments produced by someone else.

Sometimes production teams are split into even more levels, especially if the project is complicated or consists of many different parts. A supervising producer might manage one or more producers in several different productions—especially in television—either working by themselves or under the supervision of an executive producer. A coordinating producer blends together the activities of two or more individual producers who work in different but related departments in order to achieve a unified end result.

Production supervisors and production managers handle day-to-day details, negotiate business deals with the crews, and often hire the heads of various production departments. A production coordinator keeps everyone informed on progress, while a producer's assistant provides personal services to the producer. A production accountant pays the bills and keeps the financial records, also called the "books."

The Producers Guild of America (PGA) is the nonprofit trade group that represents all members of the producing team in film, television, and new media. The PGA admits that all the titles can be confusing, and the organization attempts to explain what each person does on their website.

Forming a Partnership

To handle the creative execution, the producer usually hires the director, who then takes charge of the artistic interpretation of the film or show. The director makes all the decisions that affect how the story is told and shown. The producer and director then typically team up to choose the cast and assemble the support staff.

As in the case of *Spider-Man: Homecoming*, that staff can grow to be very large and complex, depending on the scope of the project.

Numerous Divisions

People who work on a movie usually function in separate departments or crews. At the head of each department or crew is someone with certain knowledge or skills who manages other people with specialized abilities in that area. Big productions can have many different departments; smaller projects may involve fewer people, with each person handling two or more jobs.

Actors bring the script to life. They portray the characters and serve as the public image of the work that went into the production. Screenwriters tell the story, providing the script that includes dialogue and set directions that map out what the actors say and do. Cinematographers work with directors to decide the movie's "look," including the way the film will be shot, the locations they will use, and how lighting should be planned for each scene. Their staff might include a director of photography responsible for the cameras and visual appearance of the film. The composer writes the music and directs the music production for the film, while conductors and musicians record the score.

Set directors analyze the script and make sure the scenes look realistic. Art directors handle set designs, and costume designers choose or create the clothes the actors will wear. Location managers find the best scene locations and negotiate permissions with owners. They also manage aspects like catering requirements, safety, parking, and power sources. Other important staffers include makeup artists, gaffers (electricians and lighting experts), and prop masters.

After the movie has finished shooting, the editor works closely with the director to choose the final scenes and arrange them in the correct order. The sound designer handles the sound effects and manages the sound's postproduction process. The visual effects (VFX) department handles images that couldn't be filmed live on the set.

Different for TV

Television differs from the film industry in that TV projects often take the form of a series, a group of episodes with the same theme and cast. In television, an executive producer often supervises one or more producers or series; she or he may even be responsible for creating the idea or writing episodes. In television, executive producers can also be called showrunners, meaning that they control all the daily operations of a show, including producing and writing responsibilities.

Large-scale film productions can involve hundreds or even thousands of talented professionals, both in front of and behind the camera.

Sometimes a television actor becomes so important to the success of the series that he or she becomes part of the creative team and assumes a producer title. For example, in the long-running television series *24*, actor Kiefer Sutherland played leading character Jack Bauer. During the second season of the series, Sutherland added a producer title; as the series continued its run, he rose to co–executive producer and then executive producer.

Working as One

Given the size and complexity of projects, it's easy to understand the importance of the producer's role in making sure that all of the different pieces come together. World-famous filmmaker Stephen Spielberg knows that any producer's success depends on assembling the right team. "Filmmaking is all about appreciating the talents of the people you surround yourself with," Spielberg says, "and knowing you could never have made any of these films by yourself."

However, all teams need a coach to make sure that everyone works together effectively. As producer and director Ridley Scott once said, "I think, at the end of the day, filmmaking is a team, but eventually there's got to be a captain."

French brothers Auguste and Louis Lumière appear in their laboratory in 1892. They invented an early motion picture camera and produced their first movies before 1900.

CHAPTER THREE

Getting It Done

More than 120 years ago, in 1896, brothers Louis and Auguste Lumière introduced their movie *Arrival of the Train* to an audience at the Grand Café in Paris, France. The flickering black-and-white images showed just what the title suggested—a train pulling into a station, heading right toward the camera. At first, the only sound that could be heard in the room was the clatter of film feeding through the projector. Then, the audience gasped as the train sped toward them. They had never seen anything like it. The Lumière film lasted only fifty seconds, but many people believe it marked the birth of the movie business.

Big Changes

Films have certainly changed a lot since then. Silent black-and-white films ruled movie theaters until the 1930s, when sound and color introduced audiences to a whole new era of experience. When television first gained popularity in the 1950s, some filmmakers feared that television would keep people in their homes and away from films, but that didn't happen.

In fact, movies began to find a second life, moving to television after ending their run in theaters. Repurposed films and live performances became the building blocks that helped television become the force it is today.

Can you imagine how the Lumière brothers' first audience members would react if they could enter one of today's modern theaters and view the latest studio blockbuster? Recent advances in production techniques, including special effects, 3D, and CGI (computer-generated imagery), continue to add to the audience experience. As moviemaking became more complex, however, producers had to develop even more skills and manage even more responsibilities in order to successfully guide their projects from start to finish.

Stages of Production

One thing that hasn't changed? It still takes a lot of work to produce a film. Good stories, careful planning, and thoughtful management still separate profitable projects from failures. And no matter the size of a film project, all of them go through similar phases of preparation.

Generally speaking, film and television production can be split into three distinct stages: preproduction (starting the project and planning the steps), production (the actual filming or recording), and postproduction (getting it ready to be shown to an audience). Some producers consider initial development and final distribution to be so important to the process that they treat these as two additional, separate stages.

All of the hard work seems worthwhile when producers show their work to the public, such as this premiere for *Star Wars: The Last Jedi* in 2017.

What is important to remember is that these processes often overlap. Scripts get rewritten, budgets adjusted, and schedules revised. One of a producer's key qualities is the ability to remain steady yet flexible, ready to adjust course when necessary while keeping eyes focused on the final goal.

Preproduction

As mentioned earlier, all creative projects begin with a big idea or concept. Sometimes a producer comes up with it alone. In other cases, a writer will use their own idea to prepare a script and then look for a producer to organize the project and raise the money. Or a director will come up with an idea and look for both a writer and a producer to help bring it to life. If someone else owns the idea (for example, a book's author), the producer will purchase an option to use it to make the movie.

When the producer options a script, he locks in the exclusive right to present it in a certain way and for a specific period of time. The producer pays a fee to the owner to take the work off the market while he or she arranges the other necessary parts of the project, including finding investors and hiring major team members like the director and lead actors. Sometimes productions can take longer than expected, so the producer may negotiate additional option periods to extend the deadlines, with more money paid to the owner each time.

Attorney Charles Grippo has written about the legal requirements for producing films and plays. "The chief reason for [taking an option] is the money factor," Grippo says. "Until the producer can raise the necessary funds, he cannot guarantee he can produce the [project]." The producer may also need the option to convince a particular director or actor to join the crew.

Forming the Team

The producer's next step is to form a company or organization devoted to the project. That can be complicated; producers have to hire many people with very different abilities. Directors, managers, actors, artists, writers, technicians, accountants—everyone has to get involved, and their roles and personalities need to be blended together.

Producers must make sure that props, sets, and scenery match the historical period that the film portrays. These items are on the set of the 2012 movie *Lincoln*.

Many producers find that building and managing production teams is one of their favorite jobs. Producer and actor Chris Evans has said, "I like the feeling of making things … Filmmaking is that type of experience, where you're forced to collaborate with so many people. You're involved in the beginning to end, you're involved with so many elements, and when it's done, you're like, 'I made this movie.'" American actress and producer Kerry Washington feels the same: "I just really love producing. I love being able to be part of a solution. I love being able to create opportunities for other people to do what they do, to be part of the collaborative process that is filmmaking and television making."

Write It Down

If a script does not already exist, one of a producer's first jobs is to hire a screenwriter. To start, he or she will choose someone to prepare a "treatment" of the idea, a quick summary that includes short descriptions of the plot and characters as well as the major scenes and events that will take place. The screenwriter then provides a full script that includes all the dialogue and describes the actions the characters take.

Before making movies based on popular books like the *Harry Potter* series, producers must first sign agreements with the author.

Depending on the project, preproduction might include a group of researchers who study the facts and history behind the script to make sure everything makes sense. For example, a show based on historic events needs to accurately portray what happened and reflect the time period when everything took place.

In her book *Lights, Camera, Action: Making Movies and TV from the Inside Out*, author Lisa O'Brien compares a screenplay to a blueprint that builders use to plan and construct a home or skyscraper, writing that "it gives the director, the designers, makeup artists, camera people, props people, special effects people and actors a picture of the make-believe world they will create by making the movie."

It's About the Story

Los Angeles–based director Eric Nicholas wrote a book, *Picture Yourself Directing a Movie*, in which he said, "The script is the most important part of your movie. It's the foundation on which everything is built: acting, cinematic style, locations, audience reaction … everything. You can't make a great movie without a great script."

This advice can be especially important to a high-school student planning a first project. Big-budget movies with famous stars, exotic locations, and exciting special effects may be able to please audiences even without a great script. Without those distractions, however, all the viewer will really see is the story and how it's told. For student projects, the script will play the biggest role in determining whether the audience likes it.

A Valued Partner

While some people produce and direct their movies, larger projects generally require different people to fill each role. In those situations, it is likely that the producer will be looking for his or her most important collaborator very soon, if he or she hasn't already done so.

The director's vision brings the story to life, so the producer usually recruits his or her future partner at the earliest stage of the process, unless he or she is waiting for a complete screenplay before approaching a director to take over day-to-day management. In any event, the producer and director are typically both on board before they move on to the next phase of the preproduction process.

How Much Will It Cost?

Next, the producer and director will work with other key people to "break down" the script to estimate what resources will be required to complete the project. That information will help them build a budget and determine how much money they need to find to make their movie.

Shooting major motion pictures or television shows is expensive. Someone has to pay all the salaries for producers, directors, actors, composers, designers, technicians, editors, musicians, and other staff members. Sets, costumes, equipment, props, locations, and special effects all cost money; food, fuel, rent, insurance, medical coverage, and publicity charges all enter into the equation as well.

Over the years, the cost of **making movies** has ballooned as the size and scope of filmmaking have expanded. Budgets for feature films now run anywhere from just a few million dollars to $100 million, or perhaps much more. The 2011 movie *Pirates of the Caribbean: On Stranger Tides* reportedly cost nearly $410 million to make, making it the most expensive movie ever. Before anyone, or any company, commits that kind of money to make a film, they need to be convinced that it has a good chance of success.

Sales Pitch

Major studios provide most of the money for big-budget films. Producers might also recruit individual investors, usually wealthy people who have an interest in funding a film and helping it to be successful. Anyone who invests money in a project is looking to get a good return—get more out than they put in.

Sometimes producers of documentary films approach people or organizations with a strong interest in the same subject. Examples can include government agencies, religious or charitable organizations, and public interest groups.

Working together, the producer and director assemble the critical team members, including the lead actors and other key roles like a composer and a cinematographer. These essential people are often called the "package." The producer will then try to sell this collection of talent, or package, to an investor to raise the money that he or she needs to finance the project. The past success or current popularity of the team can go a long way in helping the producer

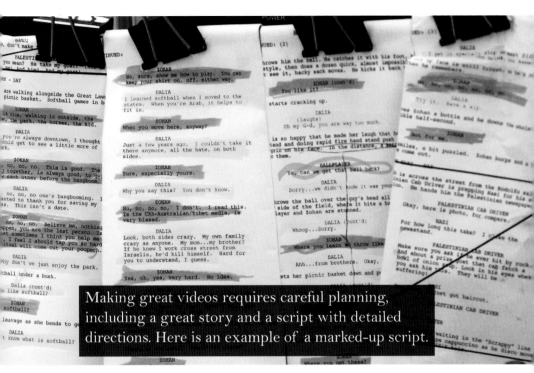

Making great videos requires careful planning, including a great story and a script with detailed directions. Here is an example of a marked-up script.

convince potential investors that the project will be a success and that they will be rewarded with a substantial profit.

Production Begins

When a producer gets the funding he or she needs to move forward—when he or she has received what is referred to as the "green light"—it's time to choose a date to begin production. This is the stage when the movie or television show actually starts being staged and filmed—or "shot." This phase is also called principal photography.

The producer works with the team to build out the shooting schedule. Every project is different, and the length of time it takes to shoot a film or show depends on the script and the budget. Major studio films often take two to six months to shoot, while films with lower budgets, as well as television shows, may take four or five weeks. It is also important to have a backup plan, since timing can be thrown off by people getting sick, bad weather, or problems with equipment.

During the production stage, a producer's main job is to keep the project on schedule and make sure that all the spending stays within budget.

Postproduction

When the movie finishes shooting, it's not done. Not by a long shot. Now, all the different elements that the film crew created must be combined and edited into a finished product. This phase often takes many months—usually much longer than the actual shooting itself.

The film editor takes the individual shots—many of them different versions of the same scene—and selects the best versions, linking them together like puzzle pieces that need to be arranged in a straight line.

First, editors prepare a "rough cut," the first version of the film that only includes live action and dialogue. They then work toward the "final" cut, which adds music, special effects, and titles. What could amount to eighty hours or more of video for a movie will eventually be edited down and organized into a final version, which runs about two hours on average.

During this period, the producer will most likely spend most of his or her time arranging for theaters to show the film, as well as beginning to promote it to the public. After all, if the audience doesn't respond, the project will be considered a failure. It's interesting to note that movie trailers that appear months in advance are often put together well before the film is actually finished with postproduction.

New Possibilities

Before the appearance of digital technology, moviemaking could be ponderous, unwieldy, and very costly. Film was expensive and hard to work with, and producers needed special cameras and projectors to shoot their projects. Anyone who wanted to enter the film business faced long odds and had to rely on finding entry-level positions to begin a years-long climb up the career ladder.

The rise of cheaper equipment like portable cameras, videotape, and digital media allowed more people to begin producing their own independent movies away from big studios. Today, internet sites like YouTube help even beginners to distribute their work to audiences around the world.

While new technology makes it easier than ever for students to produce their own projects, in many ways the process of filmmaking remains much the same. Making a good video takes more thought than simply viewing a scene and tapping the "record" button. Aspiring student producers still need to find that "big idea." Then they need to prepare a script, organize a plan, build a team, shoot their video, and arrange its distribution.

Developing Skills

To meet the challenge of actually producing a video project, students need to be well versed in a number of different skill sets. They have to be able to write well and communicate with others, so English composition and speech classes are important. They also have to understand budgets and how to spend and track money, so math, business, and economics classes play important roles as well.

Many of these skills are included in a STEM curriculum, which stresses science, technology, engineering, and mathematics. Problem-solving skills taught in STEM classes help producers to understand the many different tasks involved in film production and to appreciate the talents that potential team members may specialize in. Computer animation, financial analysis, web development (for distribution and promotion)—all these STEM-related skills have become more important than ever.

Watch and Learn

In addition to taking the right classes, many experts recommend that students interested in the field gain some perspective by, believe it or not, watching as many different movies and television shows as possible. As they do, they should pay attention to details beyond the main story—the music, sets, scenery, lighting, props, and costumes.

Matthew Goldman studied film production both in high school and at college. He currently works as

STEM classes help students learn the problem-solving, math, and technical skills they will need to successfully produce video projects.

an operations manager for a digital video and audio company and says that watching movies on DVD helped him understand how producers work. "I got interested in middle school," Goldman says. "I had a particular fascination with how films were put together. I felt like producers were the people 'behind the wall.' I used to watch DVDs and search for any extra features that included a behind-the-scenes look at how the movie was made."

Students can also read books about producing as a career and about the movie industry in general.

If possible, they should try and talk with someone actually involved in producing video projects, even from a small local company, or at least look online for interviews, articles, and blogs where producers talk about their career path and how they made it to the top.

High School Activities

While high schools may offer more opportunities to participate in live theater (plays and musicals) than film or video production, that situation is changing. Matthew Goldman remembers that his high school had just started a film class as an elective when he got there, and "through that we started a film club. We were lucky that some parents worked in the industry and could give us some insight and help teachers plan projects."

Some schools allow students to handle jobs in a student production under supervision. Since one of a producer's main jobs is attracting investors, working to raise funds for student functions or charitable causes can provide invaluable experience for contacting investors to support a video project. Students can also work on committees that organize, produce, and publicize special events, not just movies or shows. Those could take place at school, a charitable organization, or a sports league.

Volunteer Jobs

Experience in real-world productions also can help. Young people looking to learn about production often try to find positions as "go-fers" or "runners," moving around a set trying to help members of a production crew and "going for" one thing or another. Sometimes these people are called production assistants, or PAs. It's a lot of hard effort for little or no pay, but students get to work all over the set and meet (and impress) many different people in the business. Famous producer/director Steven Spielberg began his career as a PA for Universal Studios.

During his senior year of high school, Matthew Goldman worked as an intern at a company that produced food commercials. "I was just an unpaid production assistant getting coffee and water," he remembers, "but being there to witness everything was a really cool experience."

Former agent and film-career mentor Paul Duddridge suggests that students look for film and TV listings on the internet to find contact details of producers and directors who may be working on local projects. "Offer your services as an assistant or a cheap pair of hands. You will get a bite," he says.

Producer Michael Berliner suggests that students look for a mentor with some industry experience, but not necessarily a well-known name. "That way," he says, "they're not so distanced from the kind of work that you're doing that they're unable to advise you properly. But because they have been around the block before, they'll have learned things through trial and error, and can hopefully help stop you from treading into the same rabbit holes."

Making friends with lower-level assistants on productions is also a good tactic, Berliner adds, because they are the ones who hire runners. Once you have some experience under your belt, the easier it will be to get better positions.

Make a Movie

Experts agree, however, that the best way for students to learn how to produce video is "just do it." Director and actress Karen Arthur has said, "Until you make a few [movies], you haven't any proof that you can do what you think you can do."

Producers must know how to build strong teams to be successful. This group of students is learning how to develop their own film projects through hands-on experiences.

A "MARVELOUS" RISE

Kevin Feige worked his way up in the film industry to become the president of Marvel Studios, where he's produced blockbuster hits that include *Iron Man, Thor, The Avengers, Captain America: The First Avenger, Guardians of the Galaxy, Spider-Man: Homecoming*, and *Black Panther*.

As a teenager in New Jersey, Feige knew he wanted to work in Hollywood. After high school, he applied to the University of Southern California (USC) School of Cinematic Arts because his favorite

Marvel President Kevin Feige (*far right*) began his career as an intern (pictured with director Jon Watts, actor Tom Holland, and producer Amy Pascal).

directors went there. USC rejected his application five times, but Feige kept trying and was finally accepted.

Feige got his start in the movie business when he landed a job as an intern with producer Lauren Shuler Donner. His first duties included teaching actress Meg Ryan how to use email on the set of *You've Got Mail* in 1998. When Donner began work on the *X-Men* movies in 2000, she made Feige an associate producer because he knew so much about the Marvel characters on which the movies were based.

In a profile for *Vanity Fair* magazine, Joanna Robinson wrote that "Feige's innovative, comic-book-based approach to blockbuster moviemaking— having heroes from one film bleed into the next—has changed not only the way movies are made but also pop culture at large."

Feige stresses the importance of being flexible as a producer: "We change things every day when new and better ideas come along, or when an idea in a movie that is currently filming will somewhat impact a movie that's still in development."

"The easiest way to get into the industry is to make something. Anything," says Paul Duddridge. "Just start. Shoot anything at all, even on your phone. Even the edit software is included in your laptop." Then enter your film into every film festival you can find, he adds. "I'm a huge fan of high-concept, low-budget as an attention getter."

You should also reach out to people your own age who have the same ambitions as you, says Niyi Akeju, learning campaigns manager at the British Academy of Film and Television Arts. "We often find that up-and-coming craftspeople have collaborated with those at the same experience level as themselves to get their first breaks," she says.

Recording live video interviews can help students gain valuable production experience.

A big advantage for today's beginners is that they don't need big, expensive, hard-to-master equipment to make a movie or show. Phones, digital cameras, or camcorders are easy to use, and recording space is virtually limitless and cheap. Keep experimenting and, if you don't like your first results, try again and use what you have already learned. Digital software can help you edit and finalize your project, and a big-screen TV can simulate a movie theater to premiere your production.

Many smartphones include high-quality, digital cameras, totally portable, that can record "TV-ready" video and sound in all kinds of conditions and lighting. Independent filmmaker Robert Blofield has written that "for the first time ever, it really doesn't matter what equipment you have available to you—anyone can make a movie."

Come Up With a Plan

So how should you start your first film project? In his book *Picture Yourself Directing a Movie*, author Eric Nicholas suggests that student filmmakers start by asking themselves some questions. "What message or theme am I passionate about?" Nicholas writes. "What kind of story and characters will get people interested? What will make my project stand out from all the others?" Do you want to work on your own, or invite some friends to brainstorm with you?

Robert Blofield recommends that students "make a habit of taking video or photos of anything that interests you. Write down any ideas that come to you in a notebook or phone app. Practicing these skills will make you the best filmmaker you can be." Perhaps you can build a story around a subject or activity you already know—a hobby, sport, activity, or something that you heard or experienced that you think might inform or entertain others.

Once you decide what project to pursue, your next step should be to create a storyboard or outline. Divide the story into major parts—how does it begin? How does it end? Then, plan scenes for each part. You can make drawings or models to portray what you want to put on video.

Keep It Short

Many professionals recommend starting small, at least in the beginning. Limit your project to ten minutes or less. The more you include, the more that can go wrong or the more complicated it can get. That can be frustrating for beginners. If you produce a successful short film that you can show quickly and get a positive reaction, you will be even more excited to use your experience to take on more complicated and longer projects.

See How You Did

When you finish your video and like the results, arrange a showing at your house or at a local school or library. Nothing provides better feedback than watching the reactions of a live audience.

You can also upload your project to online sites like YouTube, or look to enter local contests. Many

Experts recommend that students start out with short and simple projects.

exist, and some focus on beginning filmmakers. Other competitions might include advanced submissions from more experienced producers, but even these can provide good opportunities to meet others with similar interests or who have complementary skills that can help you produce your next project.

Producers need to navigate any problems they encounter during a project, including bad weather. Here actor Leonardo DiCaprio drives a car through rain while filming *Inception*.

CHAPTER FOUR

Overcoming Obstacles

Sometimes life does not go as smoothly as you'd like. You've prepared for a test but then questions appear about topics that you didn't expect. A writing assignment takes longer than you thought it would, or you get caught in the rain when the weather forecast called for a sunny day. Perhaps you are looking forward to getting together with your friends, but then a sudden conflict leads to uncomfortable relationships and awkward conversations. Or you've spent too much money this month and can't afford to buy a ticket to the concert that everyone is going to.

Whatever problems we face, we manage to get through them. In fact, we often learn something from the experience that helps us avoid a similar result in the future. Perhaps we can plan our day better or watch our spending more closely, or be more careful in what we say to avoid hurting someone else's feelings.

Same Lessons

Producers often experience those same kinds of issues as they work on their projects. In fact, because producers are involved in all phases of the operation from beginning to end, their problems tend to be even more complicated as they try to bring a movie or television project to the screen.

Obstacles that producers deal with on a regular basis can include:

- Ideas that just don't work out after showing initial promise.

- Personal conflicts between members of the crew, resulting either from disagreements about how things should be done or simply due to different personalities and the pressure of the job.

- Unplanned absences due to sickness or unexpected circumstances, especially if other people depend on the person who is missing.

- Less-than-ideal set conditions, including rain, wind, and poor crowd control during outdoor filming. Cloudy skies can affect lighting as well, and less daylight during winter months can influence shooting schedules.

- Problems with locations you've selected for filming, including denied permits, limited access, and noise coming from unexpected sources.

- Unusual requirements for costumes, clothes, or props to accurately reflect the time period, location, or theme of the project.

- Cost overruns, including unanticipated expenses due to damaged equipment or schedule delays.

When Everything Went Wrong

Perhaps nothing personifies how badly things can go for a producer than what happened during the filming of *Apocalypse Now*, Francis Ford Coppola's controversial 1979 movie about Vietnam. Many consider *Apocalypse Now* to be the most difficult project in film history.

Coppola produced, co-wrote, and directed *Apocalypse Now*. During preproduction, many prominent actors declined Coppola's offer to play the main role, including Steve McQueen, Jack Nicholson, Robert Redford, and Al Pacino—leading actors of the day. Coppola hired Harvey Keitel, only to fire him a short time later. Martin Sheen then took the lead, but he was struggling at the time with personal issues, including alcohol. Another famous actor, Marlon Brando, showed up badly overweight and totally unprepared for his role; he hadn't even read the script before arriving on the set. The situation would soon get much, much worse.

Apocalypse Now was filmed in the Philippines and was plagued with problems throughout the shoot. Coppola kept making changes to the script, which led to a lot of wasted time for the crew. Many of the actors quarreled with each other and with Coppola. Some refused to appear on the set at the same time. Sheen later suffered a near-fatal heart attack during filming, causing further delays. Coppola also got in trouble with local officials for shooting certain scenes without permission, and to top it off, a typhoon destroyed all the sets, which had to be rebuilt.

Coppola had originally planned to shoot *Apocalypse Now* in six weeks, but it wound up taking sixty-eight. The project was further delayed as thousands of feet of film needed to be compiled and edited. Coppola also had trouble choosing the ending; he had written and filmed several different versions and could not decide which one to use.

Apocalypse Now cost about $32 million to make, a huge sum at that time. Coppola invested millions of his own money and eventually had to mortgage his home and vineyards to complete the project.

Worth It

While *Apocalypse Now* received mixed reviews when it opened, it did well at the box office and even received nominations for Best Picture at both the Academy Awards and the Golden Globe Awards. Today, many people consider *Apocalypse Now* to be one of the greatest films ever made. In 2000, the film was selected for preservation in the National Film Registry by the Library of Congress for being "culturally, historically or aesthetically significant." In 2009, the London Film Critics' Circle voted *Apocalypse Now* the best movie of the last thirty years.

The story behind *Apocalypse Now* teaches two very valuable lessons. First, successful production depends on blending all the elements into a solid plan that anticipates as many issues as possible. Second, even if unexpected problems seem insurmountable, a producer with passion and determination can weather the storm and still deliver a successful, rewarding project.

A Good Start

There's an old saying that states that successful projects begin by following the rule of the "Five P's": Proper Planning Prevents Poor Performance. Perhaps it's no coincidence that the title of "producer" and the word "project" also start with the letter "p." Good planning helps any video production get off on the right foot.

Simon Cade is an English filmmaker and director who runs a YouTube channel called DSLRguide, which is a resource for filmmakers on all levels with advice on what he calls the art of making movies. In an instructional video on his website, Cade talks about the importance of planning:

> When you're making a film, it's tempting to rush into shooting—without a script, without organizing anything. So when it's time to start filming, everything is a bit of a mess, and time is wasted picking up the pieces. If we had spent some time planning every aspect of the film, especially the creative side, then when it comes to production, everything happens a bit more smoothly and quickly.

Marina Bruno began her movie career at a young age. Following in her filmmaker father's footsteps,

Sometimes producers will have to negotiate arguments or conflicts that happen between people.

Bruno made her first official short film at sixteen. She then founded her own production company and produced several short films that became popular online. At the age of nineteen, Bruno wrote, directed, produced, and edited her first feature film. She continues to create new works, which have been showcased on her YouTube channel as well as shown in several film festivals across the globe.

Bruno advises young producers that "it's incredibly important to be prepared when making a movie, but oftentimes new filmmakers make this mistake because they don't know what to prepare for. The list is long," Bruno says, "but the most important things are: have lots of charged batteries, account for your gear/costumes/supplies, check the weather, finalize any permits/permissions, and wear comfy shoes."

Questions to Ask

Young producers can help ensure the success of their projects by starting off with some basic "did you" questions. For example:

- Did you start off with a good idea?

- Did you map out the project in enough detail to make a good estimate about how much time it would take and how much it would cost?

- Did you make a list of what equipment you would need and who you could ask to help you?

- Did you make sure that the people helping you were ready to commit their energy and time to the project?

- Did you check to make sure that you had the legal right to use any music, videos, or links from other sources that you put in your project?

Simon Cade admits, however, that planning is never perfect. "Something is still bound to go wrong, and that's what makes it interesting."

Share Information

Albert Dupont is the advanced TV broadcasting facilitator (teacher) at the Satellite Center in Luling, Louisiana, part of the St. Charles Parish Public School System located near New Orleans. Dupont believes that producers who organize their projects will face fewer problems, and that it's the producer's job to get everyone on the same page before the production starts. He suggests that his student producers hold a meeting to help their team understand what is expected from them, regardless of the type of project.

"If it's a studio production, such as a news broadcast or talk show, come up with a written show rundown and give everyone on the crew a copy," Dupont recommends. "Even if it's a sporting event, you should also have a rundown. The live event rundown may not be as detailed as the news show, but it should have a plan on how to handle pre-game, going to breaks, half-time and the end of the game. All of this information needs to be shared with the entire crew."

A Productive Meeting

For most projects, running a good production meeting includes many steps. Producers should prepare for the meeting beforehand and provide a checklist of what's being covered to all who attend. If there's a script, everyone should receive a copy. Prospective shooting dates and times should be discussed to make sure everyone will be available. Alternate dates can also be blocked out in case something goes wrong, like bad weather, illness, a surprise exam, or a family trip.

The producer can also ask each person about their interests and abilities, after which he or she can assign jobs and responsibilities for things like props, costumes, and transportation. It's also always a good idea to ask someone to take written notes since the producer will be busy running the meeting. The notes can be distributed afterward so everyone remembers what was discussed and what they agreed to.

What is important to remember is that, if one phase of a project is not completed correctly, it will have to be redone later. That will cause delays, which could lead to frustration and possible failure.

Divide Responsibilities

If two different people will be serving as producer and director, it's especially important for these key people to fully understand their relationship and where each person's responsibilities lie. Directors usually handle the creative approach and vision of the movie or show. Most directors want the producer to facilitate the project while staying in the background and out of the artistic process.

Plan the Money

Part of the planning process for any project includes building a realistic estimate about how much everything will cost and figuring out where the money will come from.

Movie studios and investors can spend millions to create, market, and distribute a major film. For big projects like these, financial analysts use their STEM skills to work with the production team to create a budget. They predict what the total costs are going to be for all aspects of the project from start to finish, often using computer-generated models to analyze different ways that they can make the movie.

They may make choices to keep costs low, such as using less expensive equipment, traveling less, scheduling fewer work days with longer hours, or using computer-generated images instead of real scenes and actors. Once the budget is set and production begins, financial analysts constantly review expenses and prepare reports that compare estimated costs and budgets to what is actually being spent.

A high-school student may spend only a small amount on a project, but it's likely that those dollars will be just as precious, especially if the producer is spending his or her own money. Underestimating the costs of the video or failing to collect on commitments from others who agreed to share the expenses can stop any project dead in its tracks.

Agree on Costs

Meg McHutchison has worked independently for more than fifteen years as a video producer and director. Many of her projects involve making promotional films for nonprofit companies. McHutchison says that one of her most important jobs is to make sure that she and the client are on the same page in terms of how much the project will cost.

"Usually the most difficult part is working with clients who don't understand the medium or how much money, time, and effort it requires to complete a project," McHutchison says. "We need to educate our clients to understand that if you choose to include certain elements, it affects the budget. People don't see that relationship, or don't understand that after certain review points it's difficult to make changes."

McHutchison believes that advance preparation is important to prevent problems and misunderstandings.

"Avoiding those pitfalls has to do with my ability to articulate the plan in the first place," she says. "The client needs to agree to the script, storyboards, budget, and schedule, those key components. In postproduction, there's a lot of detail involved in editing and graphics generation that's hard for people to understand. What they see is a thirty-second segment, but it's taken twenty-five hours for someone to do it."

Don't Be Surprised

John Kenrick, who has worked as a producer, director, and scriptwriter, writes that "no matter how well you plan, there is no way to foresee every contingency. 'Little surprises' are bound to crop up ... [and] then there are some far more costly surprises ... and you have no time for additional fundraising when you're in the heat of production."

Kenrick recommends that "it is best to expect the unexpected ... This is why I advise having an emergency fund equal to ten percent of your total budget. That will cover most surprise expenses, and odds are you will not need all of it."

Know the Rules

In addition to managing creativity, people, logistics, and money, producers also have to make sure that they follow all applicable regulations and laws. Rules can be complicated and can affect everything from handling staff contracts and local permits to taking out accident insurance policies and acquiring the rights to use other people's work.

Attorney Charles Grippo explains that "every time a producer does anything, it has legal consequences." Producers negotiate contracts with staff members, landlords, managers, and suppliers. They must also understand all kinds of different legal structures and requirements for raising and managing finances. Grippo adds, "Once [the producer] raises money, he's responsible for how it gets used."

Borrow with Permission

Students in particular need to be aware of one crucial legal requirement that, if misunderstood, can lead to serious problems for beginning filmmakers: copyrights. Copyrights are regulations that concern the use of intellectual property. They protect original works of artists, writers, and musicians. These can include books, photos, and videos, as well as songs and computer animations.

Digital technology makes it easy to discover and copy someone else's creative work and include it in new projects that may be posted online for others to see. However, the rules for using this material can be complicated. For example, students may be allowed to include a snippet of a famous song, but not the entire song. Producers need to make sure that they follow "fair use" regulations and have the right to use other people's creations if they intend to include them in their own project.

BOUNCING BACK

After graduating from Brown University, Nina Jacobson built an impressive career as a senior film executive and producer at companies like DreamWorks, Universal, and Disney, where she served as president of Walt Disney Motion Picture Group. Jacobson's many achievements included the first *Pirates of the Caribbean* movie as well as *Remember the Titans* and the first *Chronicles of Narnia* film.

Despite her successes, Jacobson was fired in 2006 as part of a management shake-up. Rather than be discouraged, Jacobson formed her own production company, Color Force, in 2007. She took the name from a scientific term that describes the invisible force that holds microscopic particles together. "It's definitely a tough blow to your morale to get fired," Jacobson told the *Hollywood Reporter* in an interview. "People were pretty nice to me and rooting for me to dust myself off and assume a new role. I had people in my corner, but it still was scary … I was a little bit intimidated … I made sure to surround myself with people who had done it a lot more than I had."

Jacobson's company quickly secured the rights to Jeff Kinney's *Diary of a Wimpy Kid* books and successfully released three films based on the series. She then hit the jackpot by producing the *Hunger Games* series, and she also produced *The People v. O.J. Simpson: American Crime Story*, a hugely popular and critically acclaimed TV series for the FX network.

Legal Consequences

Just because you think your work is protected under the fair use regulations does not mean that the owner of the copyrighted content cannot sue you. They may try to get your video taken down or even contact you for payment. If you want to use material produced by other people in your video and are not 100 percent sure about whether it's covered under fair use, you should talk with a lawyer.

Practice First

Planning … budgeting … legal issues … students can certainly feel intimidated about trying to make their own videos, especially if they intend to work with a team. Albert Dupont encourages his students to practice new skills until they are comfortable, and he tries to provide constructive feedback and support during that process.

After everyone has had a chance to try all of the production jobs, Dupont says, "I let them 'gravitate' to the jobs they like best. That's when the producer and director types step up to the challenge and I tend to step back and watch them shine. But I am always on standby, ready to 'foam the runway' for any rough landings."

The Film School Dilemma

For high-school students already planning a career in video production, another question they may face is whether to attend a college that specializes in film and television production. While high-school students can learn a lot about making videos working on their own personal projects, many experts believe that this early practical experience should then be bolstered by specialized instruction in film school.

Each year, the *Hollywood Reporter* ranks the top twenty-five film schools in America based on feedback from educators, alumni, and industry pros. In 2017, the USC (University of Southern California) School of Cinematic Arts topped their list, followed by the film programs at New York University (NYU), the University of California at Los Angeles (UCLA), the American Film Institute in Los Angeles, and Columbia University in New York.

These and other colleges offer specialized curriculums and majors in filmmaking that emphasize skills that producers need to know, including creative development, scriptwriting, scheduling, budgeting, promotion, and team-building.

Some industry veterans strongly believe in the value of film school; others are not so sure.

The Pluses

Filmmaker Pete Shaner has written and directed two independent films and also teaches digital video production and techniques. Shaner believes that film school "provides resources and experiences you can't get anywhere else."

"Film school teaches you more than cameras and software," Shaner says. "It teaches you the professional approach for everything from lighting to editing to sound. It gets you thinking about telling stories with pictures in a different way and provides access to people and experiences you can't get anywhere else."

Paul Peditto is an award-winning screenwriter and director. He is also an adjunct professor of screenwriting at Columbia College and Second City in Chicago, Illinois. In his book *The DIY Filmmaker*, Peditto talks about how college courses can help someone learn the skills necessary to make movies:

> *When I was making my first movie,* Jane Doe, *I had no previous experience of being on a film set and so, I made all kinds of mistakes ... Had I been to film school, I might have had a clue in terms of film set responsibilities ... If I'd had formal training the chances of my first movie failing would have been reduced significantly ... You might find that the third or fourth skill you learned in film school is the one with which you'll actually make a living ... Learn as much as possible about the craft of making movies.*

A Different View

Others believe that film school doesn't have all the answers. Many successful producers and directors never attended film school, including James Cameron, Christopher Nolan, and Quentin Tarantino.

Producer Michael Berliner never went to film school and had "basically zero knowledge" of the industry when he started out. Berliner believes that making a low-budget film and finding a mentor can help students learn important filmmaking skills without attending a formal college program. "Be prepared to face some hard work and a steep learning curve," Berliner says.

Digital operations manager Matthew Goldman did attend film school. He believes that helped him because "some skills are very hard to teach in the job—people you work with do not have the time to teach you and there is just so much you can pick up." On the other hand, Goldman says, "Some production methods that they teach you in school are done a different way by companies in the real world," so practical experience is key. Goldman also recommends that students take business courses, perhaps even as a double major.

Make Connections

One thing that film school can provide is business contacts after graduation. Goldman says that it's extremely difficult to break into the video production business, and networking can play a huge role: "You have to be persistent and know what you want and make as many contacts as you can. You need to call studios or small production companies and just keep asking. You also have to network—find parents and friends that know someone in the industry. Sometimes the only way to get in is through someone who knows someone else." Goldman recommends that students choose film schools with great alumni networks to help with the job hunt after graduation.

Learning from Failure

While experts may disagree on the value of film school, they unanimously recommend that students produce their own videos and "just do it." They also remind students that their first projects will be learning experiences. Some lessons will be positive, but others may be negative. The important thing is to realize that not everything will go smoothly in the beginning, so students should not get discouraged when some elements do not go as well as they hoped.

Many successful professionals in any field, including movies and television, remember that their most difficult experiences turned out to provide their most important lessons and motivations for the future.

Lorraine Grula worked for years in Nashville, Tennessee, as a producer, camerawoman, and videotape editor before she began teaching TV production at a high school. Grula's students work on many video projects throughout the year. While most turn out well, Grula admits that other projects don't, and that students have to learn how to handle failure and criticism from others. "That happens!" she says. "As a teacher, I helped them deal with it. I helped them realize that they could NEVER satisfy everybody, nor could they ever be perfect. Learning those simple lessons is a huge leap in maturing into an adult. So teaching video production includes those kind of valuable life lessons as well."

Following a written plan and keeping good notes help producers organize and communicate with their partners.

Stay Passionate

Vince Gilligan, the creator and producer of the television series *Breaking Bad*, believes that producers can overcome problems by remembering how excited they get when they start a project. "Passion can help carry you through the times when it seems as though no one believes in you or your project but you," Gilligan says. "It can keep you focused long enough to actually overcome the odds and find a way to finish your film. It can get you back inside your head to imagine another project waiting to be realized … [and] will help you get to the finish line when you've run out of the will to keep going."

Camcorders and smartphones make it easier than ever for students to produce their own movies.

CHAPTER FIVE

Real-Life Careers

Working on successful video projects can provide enormous professional and personal satisfaction, but a producer's life may not be right for everyone. Luckily, high-schoolers who get involved in video production learn many skills that easily translate to other fields. This can work whether you choose another career right after graduation or if you decide to reinvent yourself after working as an actual producer.

Valued Skills

Anyone who has produced a video project, whether large or small, has already gotten a head start on building career success. Producers hire and coordinate the entire crew, gaining valuable management and team-building experience that most companies seek. Producers also have to communicate well, both with their own staff as well as with their superiors, moderators, suppliers, and the media. They have to troubleshoot and solve problems, and they have to be able to understand finances, make budgets, and manage money.

Producers must also be comfortable dealing with creative and technical areas, which are very different. They need to recognize a good story and be able to promote it in a way that's meaningful to an audience or a business client. Video technology is also changing at a rapid pace, and producers need to keep up-to-date and adapt so they can take advantage of what the latest developments have to offer.

Many Choices

When high-school students begin to work on video projects, they often find that one particular area interests them more than others. Learning about different jobs may help students choose a career path down the road, says Kay Verdon, careers manager at Creative Skillset. "Research, research, research—find out about the different job roles out there," she says.

Nicola Lees, a talent agent and career mentor, agrees that learning about all the producer's responsibilities, including planning, scripts, lighting, sound, and logistics, serves as a great introduction to other careers. She says, "I love writing, but found my niche in writing proposals for TV programs rather than screenwriting. That brought me a regular income, the opportunity to dip into lots of interesting worlds, and also sit at the table with [producers] in pitch sessions, which was an amazing experience."

Try Everything

When he was young, Yaniv Kanfi wanted to be a filmmaker and play lead guitar in a rock band. He received his bachelor's degree in fine arts from New York University with a major in film production/cinematography. While he was in college, Kanfi says, he embraced the idea of being "a generalist" and learning about all the different things a producer has to do. "My first class in film school was a five-week crash course in independent film production where crews of four students wrote, directed, and edited five short films," Kanfi remembers. "We filled every role on a film set: actor, script supervisor, cinematographer, gaffer, art director, boom operator, sound operator, craft service, production assistant, and general gopher … I really loved doing it all, and I loved how pulling all of the disparate disciplines together into one cohesive vision creates a distinct point of view."

Attractive Mix

Deborah Mitchell is a multimedia producer who managed television projects from the concept stage until their successful on-air launch. After leaving

Many student producers have used their leadership skills to pursue success in other fields outside of television and film.

television, Mitchell entered the world of social media. She now runs the company she founded, Deborah Mitchell Media Associates, where she helps people and companies create customized websites. She also manages their social media profiles and connects them with digital influencers.

In an article for entrepreneur.com, Mitchell talks about how companies increasingly expect their employees to perform many different duties, an area where producers excel. "Producers have extensive experience wearing many hats and juggling several balls at one time and dealing with all types of people," she writes.

Building Teams

After working in television production and teaching it in high school, Lorraine Grula founded a web business concentrating on video production. Based on her experience working with students, Grula believes that "learning to make video is one of the best activities for kids that I know. Having taught both high-school and elementary-school students TV production, I can say with certainty that participating in the process of video making builds children up in a wide variety of ways."

Grula believes that making videos provides students with knowledge they will use no matter what career they choose. Students learn to put teams together and cooperate with others, she says: "Parents often turn to sports for giving teamwork experience to children. Video production is another great avenue most folks never consider. Some of my most successful student video producers were kids who were not athletic, so video was one of the few ways for them to succeed on a team."

Andrew Schmertz agrees. Schmertz is a former television executive producer who now runs Hopscotch Air, a small-plane air-taxi service. Schmertz believes that production skills help business leaders "involve your staff in the production of the entire program and encourage employees to ask for help and guidance from each other [and] include people in the decision-making process."

Running Things

Deborah Mitchell believes that experience in producing helps prepare a student for the top spot in a company. "Producing a show is a lot like founding and running a business," Mitchell says. "You need a message, a team, content or service, and great execution … Producers have carefully honed skills that are particularly suited for businesses and brands. We are excellent big-picture leaders, storytellers, and managers who are trained to work under extraordinary pressure."

Kanfi agrees. "A small, film-school style crew has to fire on all cylinders, all the time," he says. "And when it doesn't—when the team doesn't communicate, when someone isn't pulling their weight, when the unexpected inevitably happens—the only measure of success is how the team pulls through and how its leader helped negotiate resolution. Running a company is exactly like that."

Planning for Success

Lorraine Grula believes that learning to set goals and plan projects is another benefit to being a producer: "When I took [my students] through the process of deciding what to create, we began with the end goal in mind," Grula says. "What kind of show did they want to make? Funny? Dramatic? Realistic? Fantasy? Decide that first. When making video, the goal of the course is to complete a finished show. Since video making is a process, there are lots of little goals along the way. So when I teach video production, I make sure everyone realizes what small goal we are working on at the moment. Reaching all your small goals one after the other leads to reaching your large goal in the end."

For some of their video projects, Grula asked her students to set up interviews outside of the classroom. "This required advanced planning, telephoning, and scheduling," she said, and it was "a great way for them to gain poise and become confident presenting themselves."

Managing the Bottom Line

Businesses need to spend money wisely and run efficiently, and Mitchell maintains that producers excel at managing resources. "Shows are notorious for wanting a lot of production with little resources. Producers know how to stick to a budget. If we cannot afford something, then we can probably negotiate a deal to get whatever is needed in even the most unusual situations … Producers understand the value of time, money, and meeting a deadline."

Nicola Lees suggests that a producer's ability to manage budgets and arrange for shooting schedules easily translates to nonfilm careers like accounting, finance, and event planning.

Understanding Technology

As novice producers continue to experiment with new digital and web-based tools, many people in the field believe that this kind of exposure opens up a wealth of new career choices. Grula says, "With video editing, kids will learn all kinds of computer skills, many of which can easily be translated into other computer programs."

Avi Kohl graduated Brooklyn College with a bachelor of arts degree in film production. After working in that field, Kohl says, he realized that "it wasn't really the right calling for me. Years later, I discovered 3D animation through a freeware program." Kohl combined his film experience with his

Students find that digital media experience helps both inside and outside the classroom.

newfound passion for 3D graphics and joined the staff of The Animation Project, which prepares digital media programs for youth therapy groups at high schools, juvenile detention centers, and foster-care facilities.

From Film to Digital

Yaniv Kanfi also found a career in technology. In order to help pay for film school and his living expenses, Kanfi began to build software for small businesses and became, in his words, a "designer-developer-business analyst-project manager-CFO-collections agent."

Instead of going into the film business after college, Kanfi decided to stick with the technology field. He now serves as president of iTriage, which uses smart technology to give people information so they can better manage their health. Kanfi also founded DMZ Digital, which provides digital consulting services for clients.

Kanfi credits his college training in video production for exposing him to management techniques that help him every day in his business. One of the most important, Kanfi says, was learning how to identify highly skilled people: "Knowing what it takes to put together a film from every perspective allowed me to identify, empathize with, and fundamentally revere talent."

Changing Careers

No career choice has to be permanent. Some people who pursue jobs in the video industry later have a change of heart. Even if that happens, many believe that their training in film or video production still provided a valuable foundation as they decided to follow a new direction in their professional life.

New Yorker Ellie Lotan attended film school in Edinburgh, Scotland, before returning home to work in the film industry. She remembers using networking and sources like Craigslist to get work mostly as an assistant on all kinds of projects, including films, commercials, music videos, and documentaries. After six years, however, she says, "I finally admitted to myself that while I once had a dream to become a filmmaker, the reality of the industry was a completely different landscape than I had imagined. I realized that if I was to be happy, my work needed to involve compassion."

Lotan decided to leave the film industry and use the skills she learned, including storytelling and the arts, to enter the field of expressive arts therapy, which uses visual art, music, drama, dance, poetry, and creative writing for psychotherapy, counseling, rehabilitation, and medicine. She entered the master's program at the California Institute of Integral Studies in San Francisco, California, and "couldn't be prouder of the path that brought me here."

Giving Back

Sometimes even veteran producers with many years of success decide that the time has come to devote their experience to a new passion.

In 1980, Sherry Lansing became the first woman in the film industry to oversee all levels of a studio's production when she was appointed president of production at 20th Century Fox. She later ran the

CHANGING THE GAME

After graduating from USC's School of Cinematic Arts, Chanel Summers chose a career designing and producing video games. Recruited by Microsoft in the late 1990s, she was responsible for releasing their first multiplayer internet game, *Fighter Ace*, which helped fuel the rise of online gaming. Summers also served as an original member of the Xbox team, specializing in designing and supporting its audio capabilities.

Summers then left Microsoft and cofounded Syndicate 17, an audio production house that creates music and audio for films, television, commercials, and games. Summers frequently lectures around the world at music, technology, and educational events, and she serves as director of the Experimental Audio Design Lab back at her alma mater, USC.

In 2013, Summers teamed with fellow USC alumnus Kevin Bachus to establish the Bachus-Summers Fund for Innovation in Interactive Entertainment at USC's School of Cinematic Arts Interactive Media & Games Division (IMGD). The fund supports promising students in the emerging fields of interactive and immersive media.

"I've seen firsthand that the most meaningful work is always achieved when visionaries take risks and break boundaries," said Summers. "Creative and talented individuals must be allowed to realize their dreams, regardless of resources. When thinking about this fund, it was critical to us that it be used directly to support the efforts of tomorrow's creative and entrepreneurial leaders."

Motion Picture Group at Paramount, where she released more than two hundred films, including Academy Award winners *Forrest Gump, Braveheart,* and *Titanic.*

In 2005, Lansing decided to leave Hollywood at age sixty to set up the Sherry Lansing Foundation, a nonprofit organization dedicated to cancer research, health, public education, and finding new career opportunities for veteran workers. Among her foundation's initiatives is a program that retrains retired and midcareer technology professionals to serve as math and science teachers in California public schools.

Asked why she left the film business, Lansing answered that "there's a Harvard Business School thing that says, 'Every ten years you should replant yourself,' and the only way to keep young is to learn new things and keep curious." Lansing added that "from the time I was pretty young, I always thought that if I was lucky enough to achieve my dreams and if I had financial security, at a certain point in my life I wanted to give back. I wanted, just corny as it sounds, to try and make the world a better place."

A Student Advantage

It may seem hard to believe, but in some ways today's students hold the upper hand over more experienced producers who have been in the business for years. Some people think that technology is changing the way that people view movies and television so fast that younger people, who are more comfortable with digital media, will be better able to recognize new possibilities.

Producer, writer, and director Paul Peditto has written, "What's new in the game is digital technology [to shoot] a movie saying *exactly* what you want to say, and maintaining control of both content and distribution. Also new are digital platforms to sell your product that didn't exist ten years ago."

In his 2017 book *Live Cinema and Its Techniques*, Francis Ford Coppola writes about how live streaming performances and virtual reality may even change the way that people think about film and television:

> *Since the early 1990s, the cinema has transformed itself from a photochemical-mechanical medium to an electronic-digital one ... The cinema is now just about wholly digital ... I have to believe that this change will profoundly influence the essence of cinema ... taking us in new directions. What will these new directions be?*

> *In the digital world, moviemaking can now be performed ... collaborating on the internet, using game pads, joysticks, keyboards and touch screens, all the devices of internet gaming ... Virtual reality, with its point-of-view perception of the main characters, may create new formats; and movies themselves may be performed live, shown at theaters, in community centers, and in homes around the world. Eventually "cinema auteurs"*

may emerge who can use this new format
to create literature at its highest level, in
ways I cannot yet imagine.

Coppola believes that the power in these new tools may broaden the definition of a producer's role to the point that anyone with imagination and organizational skills will be able to manage all aspects of their own projects, incorporating video, audio and special effects, and distributing their videos across the internet outside of traditional models.

Breaking In

Some signs indicate that opportunities to break into video production may be expanding. It's easier for producers to shoot and distribute their own content, and streaming networks like Netflix and Amazon continue to feed the public's appetite for original programming. In truth, however, it's still difficult to gain a foothold in the industry.

Hands-on experience, past successes, and good contacts will continue to play perhaps the biggest roles in becoming a successful producer. Laura Berlinsky-Schine works as a marketing manager for Penguin Random House Publishers and also writes for CollegeVine, an online college counseling resource for high-school students. In an article, Berlinsky-Schine notes that students need to actively seek out hands-on film production opportunities:

If your high school offers film production
courses, this is an obvious place to start.

You might also take related courses, such as film appreciation or film theory. Since filmmaking involves numerous other skills, courses in related areas such as art, photography, music, acting, public speaking, and so on are good topics to pursue as well. They will help you expand your knowledge base in ways that may be applicable to film production.

Berlinsky-Schine also recommends looking into filmmaking clubs, or related activities like drama and photography clubs. If not, she says, "Start your own! If you want to gain some leadership experience and fill a niche that is not yet available in your school, look into creating your own film club. Immersive summer camps may have options for filmmaking as well. [Or] try exploring your interest in film production independently. You could start by just making short movies with your friends … Think about how you will demonstrate what you have accomplished to colleges."

Loving It

In his book *Making Movies*, John Russo talks about the uncertainty involved in video production: "Moviemaking is not only an adventure, it's a crapshoot. One can never be entirely sure how any particular project will turn out."

However, that sense of challenge and adventure is also what keeps producers coming back to their craft, time and time again. Joss Whedon has experienced

While television and film producers must master many skills to make videos, many find that their greatest satisfaction comes from building teams that share their success.

great success producing, directing, and writing for film and television. When asked to describe what he loves most about producing, Whedon compared it to another of his passions: "What I do like is hiking. And that's what filmmaking is. It's a hike. It's challenging and exhausting, and you don't know what the terrain is going to be or necessarily even which direction you're going in ... but it sure is beautiful."

GLOSSARY

Academy Award A prize given annually in Hollywood by the Academy of Motion Picture Arts and Sciences for excellence in film performance and production. The award is also called an Oscar.

auteur A filmmaker who has a personal style and keeps creative control over his or her work.

box office A term that refers to all the money a movie makes when it is released. Movie tickets used to be sold from a small booth or "box office."

budget A detailed list of projected costs for a project.

CGI Computer-generated imagery that is used to create characters, scenery, and special effects.

credits Lists that appear at the beginning and end of films, shows, and video games that include names and titles for all the people involved in the production.

crew The team of people who work together to make a video project.

curriculum A set of school courses that focus on a particular area of study.

dialogue The words spoken by actors.

digital Types of electronic data such as video, audio, pictures, and text that have been formatted to be easily recorded, distributed, and played by devices like smartphones and computers.

distribution The process of making a video project available to theaters, networks, streamers, or other places where it can be seen.

documentary A film that depicts real-life or actual events.

go-fer A low-level assistant who is usually sent on errands—"go-fer (go for) this or that."

Golden Globe Award An acknowledgement and statue given by the Hollywood Foreign Press Association for excellence in film and television.

green light When a project gets enough support to move forward.

Hollywood A section of the city of Los Angeles, California, where the film industry is based.

intern A student or trainee who works, sometimes without pay, in order to gain hands-on experience.

logistics Handling the details of an operation, including arrangements for people, locations, transportation, and supplies.

option A contract with someone who owns an idea or product that guarantees exclusive rights for a specific kind of use for a certain length of time.

pitch A presentation to investors to convince them to fund a project.

prop A small object used by actors in a film, show, or play.

screenplay A formatted document for a video production containing dialogue and stage directions but no camera or editing instructions.

series A group of episodes of a television program or several films with the same theme.

shooting In video production, a term to describe the time when recording first begins until it ends.

showrunner A person who has managerial and creative control over a television show, including producing and writing responsibilities.

streaming Watching, listening to, or distributing video and audio via the internet.

studio A major entertainment company that uses its own private facilities to make movies.

treatment A few pages that describe the plot and idea for a creative project like a film or television show.

FOR MORE INFORMATION

Books

Blofield, Robert. *How to Make a Movie in 10 Easy Lessons.* Lake Forest, CA: Walter Foster Jr., 2014.

Coppola, Francis Ford. *Live Cinema and Its Techniques.* New York: Liveright Publishing Corporation, 2017.

Hughes, Michael K. *Digital Filmmaking for Beginners: A Practical Guide to Video Production.* New York: McGraw Hill Professional, 2012.

Lyons, Suzanne. *Indie Film Producing: The Craft of Low Budget Filmmaking.* Burlington, MA: Focal Press, 2012.

Peditto, Paul, and Boris Wexler. *The DIY Filmmaker: Life Lessons for Surviving Outside Hollywood.* Bellingham, WA: Self-Counsel Press: 2015.

No Film School

https://www.nofilmschool.com/about

No Film School's website features videos and advice from a worldwide community of filmmakers, video producers, and independent creatives. As their motto suggests, No Film School is "where filmmakers learn from each other—'no film school' required." The site includes a free cinematography guide and weekly podcasts.

Producers Guild of America (PGA)

http://www.producersguild.org

The Producers Guild of America is the nonprofit trade group that represents, protects, and promotes the interests of all members of the producing team in film, television, and new media.

Introduction to Filmmaking for Beginners

https://www.youtube.com/watch?v=t33owpmMTfo

Host Simon Cade explains the basics of making a short film in this brief and entertaining video.

Nina Jacobson: Motion Picture Producer

https://www.makers.com/profiles/591f25345bf62365546ecf40

In this video, producer Nina Jacobson talks about making it in Hollywood, how she reacted to being fired, maintaining creative integrity, and taking time for family.

Online Articles

"Frequently Asked Questions About Fair Use."
Google.com. https://support.google.com/youtube/
answer/6396261?hl=en.

Johnson, Nathania. "LISTEN IN: At This Washington
High School, Students Earn A's By Producing
Podcasts." the74.com. March 4, 2016. https://
www.the74million.org/article/listen-in-at-this-
washington-high-school-students-earn-as-by-
producing-podcasts.

King, Tyler A. "Where Do You Fit in the Film
Industry?" Get In Media. Accessed April 4, 2018.
http://getinmedia.com/articles/film-tv-careers/
where-do-you-fit-film-industry.

Zeke. "So What Exactly IS a Film Producer?"
New York Film Academy. June 16, 2015.
https://www.nyfa.edu/student-resources/so-what-
exactly-is-a-film-producer.

Zipin, Dina. "How Exactly Do Movies Make Money?"
Investopedia. March 1, 2018. https://www.
investopedia.com/articles/investing/093015/how-
exactly-do-movies-make-money.asp.

INDEX

Page numbers in **boldface** are illustrations

ABOUT THE AUTHOR

Gerry Boehme is an author, editor, speaker, and business consultant who loves to travel and to learn about new things. He especially enjoys talking with people who have different backgrounds and opinions.

Boehme has written books for students dealing with many subjects, including spying and surveillance in the twenty-first century, primary sources of the civil rights movement, and theater.

Boehme was born in New York City, graduated from The Newhouse School at Syracuse University, and now lives on Long Island with his wife and two children.